WORLD ON A STRING

ARROWSMITH
PRESS

World on a String

ISBN: 979-8-9915254-4-2

Boston — New York — San Francisco — Baghdad
San Juan — Kyiv — Istanbul — Santiago, Chile
Beijing — Paris — London — Cairo — Madrid
Milan — Melbourne — Jerusalem — Darfur

11 Chestnut St.
Medford, MA 02155
arrowsmithpress@gmail.com
www.arrowsmithpress.com

The seventy-second Arrowsmith book was typeset & designed by Bella Bennett
for Askold Melnyczuk & Alex Johnson in Baskerville and Mrs. Eaves

World on a String

on a

String

Gail Mazur

CONTENTS

THREE TREES

August afternoon.

Rag paper, Winsor & Newton charcoal,
blackened kneaded eraser beside you in the grass.

Three bare oak trees. You loved what you called
the spikiness of forms, agreed with Rodin

that nothing in nature is ugly.

Monumental, burnt, those trees *expressive* for you,
as close as if your charcoal had been made of them.

You loved the *susurrus* of brush on canvas,
the *sh shh* that charcoal made on paper,

you even liked ekphrastic poems (I hated them).
You'd love me writing this.

That day I asked—was it the only time I asked?—
what you'd been thinking while you drew,

and you looked at me blankly
(you'd already explained so much to me,

that day I wanted to know more,
to be inside you, inside your working mind);

What? *what?*

How you answered,
tree   tree   tree

COUPLETS

Some nights we're young again, or you are,
Or I am. We're with our son, our daughter—

Nothing missing, not quarrels, not goofy laughter.
The four of us dreamily together.

Sometimes you're painting the dogwood in the yard,
Sometimes I call out to you but I'm not heard,

Or I'll lose you in sunny ballpark crowds
Or jumbled Roman streets, and can't utter a word....

Then I'll find you—yet somehow we never touch,
The damned dreams won't grant me that much.

Are we still married? Have we become old friends?
Sometimes we're cut off, or we fade—we don't just end.

When we're together, it's never too cold or too hot,
But one of us grows older, the other, not.

INSCRIPTION

Bless you, he wrote
on his title page,
and your funny, heart

breaking poems, and
I thank my friend
who died too soon,

my very funny,
unincorporated friend.
I think he'd like it,

—*really* like it—
if I made a joke now
with the July sun

ready to laugh
with us and the tide
determined

to wash grief away,
though I'm not ready
to laugh, not yet—

but thanks, dear Tony,
for blessing me
and reminding me

how Lowell answered
when a friend asked him
how he'd *want to be*

remembered. They were
crossing the campus
he'd fled

decades before,
where his ancestors loomed,
iconic, judgmental,

and where now he taught—
two colleagues,
well-employed—

Heartbreaking,

was his reply. One word
for all the history, intelligence,
pain, and wit—

WORLD ON A STRING

—for Erna Rosenberg, 1911–2012

Thunder, and my cats, pure products of America,
go crazy at the kitchen door,
trapped, the day—which is everything—

promising nothing for them but my departure,
dry kibble in a bowl,
then me alone in the car singing Sinatra.

I've got the world on a string,
through splotching rain driving, *I've got a song that I sing,*
a hundred miles to a wedding,

and singing *Every time we say goodbye,*
thinking of you waking yesterday *how strange the change*
in your body of ghost bones,

from major to minor, from what you'd hoped would be
your last sleep, disgusted,
grousing, "Oh no! Am I *still* here?"

How strange the change from major to minor . . .
Today, I'm getting away to dunes and bay,
my old songs for company—

Every time we say goodbye, I die a little—
toward a ceremony of *I do*'s, champagne in a museum gallery,
wild rain syncopating the roof

and suddenly everything aglow, lit by sun
and some of us will leap
from our gilded chairs to gape at a double rainbow,

a vision at the window phenomenal, fugitive—
like you, also vanishing—
and in this moment I feel sure you must have died,

and I think of your befuddled friend last week
wanting to reassure you,
saying, *But Erna, God's in all of us you know,*

and you, my devout atheist, my beloved aunt,
exploding, in panic,
protesting, *Then get him the hell out of me!*

The poor woman must have been terrified,
but I could only laugh,
when, still furious on the phone, you told me

your revulsion at her idea of your ghost-bed conversion.
What we used to say proudly about you,
decades after the Joe McCarthy 50s almost broke you.

She kept the faith . . . Now, at this window, I remember
your radiant photograph
in last year's *Globe*: CENTENARIAN PROTESTS WAR,

your snowy Thursdays demonstrating with the Zinns—
no good protest
you couldn't summon exultant diehard support for—

no bullshit you wouldn't passionately excoriate—
yet no song you couldn't sing. . . .
Here at the wedding with people I hardly know,

I marvel at the two rainbows, their radiant curves
fugitive, evanescing,
a confluence of nature and enchantment—phenomenon

the half-lit gathering takes for a great romantic omen—
then, like the brave arc of your life,
my Erna, my heroine, my exemplar, utterly gone.

THE FLEA

"The flea," that's what the year-rounders call it,
rummaging through tools or bric-a-brac, then
gossiping all day at their tables in the blistering sun,
their faded beach umbrellas barely shading the tarmac.

This is what my mother did in New Hampshire
Sunday after widowed Sunday, into her eighties.
Up at dawn, her wagon packed the night before—
by noon, willing to mark down anything not to have

to rewrap and pack the whole kit and caboodle
for the sticky hundred-mile drive home....
Today, I pick up a teapot, white with a smattering
of pink and black and aqua stars, its flawed glaze—

a reject from the start—its jaunty asterisks,
its moderne form, manufactured in Syracuse
in the 'fifties, pleases me, seven starry cups
and five chipped star-studded dinner plates—

ordinary optimistic dishes, probably used by one
Cape Cod family for decades, only dings
and cracks now to tell their homely provenance,
their good usage—and keep the price down.

Not star-struck, my mother would have felt
the edges' roughness with her thumb and found
them wanting, It wouldn't have been the chips—
she treasured her miniatures, her broken "minis"—

these just weren't *her* thing. But like a ninny—
I can make something of this, can't I—I buy the lot
in her magpie memory, wrapped in old *Globes*,
for what a *cappuccino* would cost, or a Parisian mystery.

UNTITLED, FOR ALAN DUGAN

"I've got writer's block"—
your self-loathing mutter after chemo—

writer's block—
bourgeois indulgence of the pampered—

Had you finally confronted Coleridge's
indefinite indescribable terror? ...

Months later, I ask if you're working:
"Yeah, I'm making notes—*"*

notes, life-blood our good days pulse with,
Work, the only of onlies—

*

A lifetime of punishing your body—
(how you must have loathed it)—

until the body refused to collude anymore—

You were physical wreckage, still
your cauterizing intelligence not quite disabled—

and you'd never admit despair, only disgust
at your own womanish complaint—*writer's block.*

*

Kind to the young, to the marginal
(but didn't we all think ourselves "marginal"?),

dismissive to the rest of us as we hung—
you *said* so little—on your every caustic word.

*

Some of your poems you titled "Untitled Poem,"
fuck the indexers, the Ivy academics—

your lack of pretension—
or was it arrogance?—
an offering to the god of poetry—

or a thumb in His eye.

Old iguana, cold-blooded, spiny one,
could you have relished the world's disorder
but abhorred the world?

*

When a doctor warned drinking would kill you
you'd show up at my house with a 6-pack of Kaliber,

always a tough guy. I knew you were glad to see me,
even with no gun in your pocket!

Now I recite your lines to myself, still tickled
by my own imitation of your gruffness—

I loved to grunt "Dugan style"—no, "style"
isn't the word—"*Oh I got up and went to work*

and worked and came back home
and ate and talked and went to sleep"

with its un-Dugan-like volta:
Love must be the reason for the week!

*

Caustic, graceless, you were a hard man,
the least playful except—sometimes—
in your poems—

Still, poetry was no game, was it?
Art-making's a job, the worker
shows up for it.

(Your early day job at the diaphragm factory
fit your adamant refusal of the romantic.)

*

Above your desk when you died,
shelves of drafts, unfinished—and finished—

poems, each in its own faded brown envelope—
Have they been forgotten, lost, *shredded?*

Poems so singular, so unaccommodating,
writers I know would kill to steal them....

TEXAS ROACHES

That steamy night, three of them came, lugging
their amber carapaces like too old, too heavy
luggage, their "footsteps" clicking and clacking

across my borrowed bedroom's oaken floor.
Bigger than my thumbs, almost big as Santa
Monica mice, demanding from me—only a *tenant*—

their fair price. Tough as lead nails, millennial
survivors, all that term they'd clacked for snacks—
leapt to my bed, scrunched together at my hip,

snorted crumbs from my blanket and smeared
my moody Chekhov. Muse, in my credulous youth
I swore to revere all life, no matter how repellent,

how crude the nervous system. But *but*—I made
small kissing noises for Mensch, my Russian Blue,
a creature who'd eat anything tasty, living or baked,

that he could feasibly torture and devour. His step
killingly soft, his furry hind parts twitched in feline
anticipation, his teeth made hideous gnashing noises.

Oh, those mammoth roaches, I told myself, they knew
nothing of my sorrows. Houston, that night, heartless,
I rolled on my side, turned a blind eye, a deaf ear,

and slept to the feral music of my blue cat's crunching.

NOBODY FUCKS WITH ME

Lower Broadway's midnight, fifty years ago.
Rattling boom of trucks cannoning over iron plates.

In our illegal loft, the studio gone quiet;
in the loft's loft, our children sleeping....

The 19th century Lord & Taylor building,
elegant a century before on the "Ladies' Mile,"

then wholesale novelties, artists' lofts, basement
shuls, our pornographer landlord. Twenty-foot-

high ceilings, at the edge of the Garment District.
I'd lie awake, waiting to hear the *basso profundo*

boom up lower Broadway's canyon, to vibrate
in the homely dark to a deep-voiced stranger

whose defiant mantra was part protest, part
proclamation. Every night come to lead me,

his roar reverberating up the cast-iron block,
roar I wanted to bellow, to belt out with him:

*NOBODY FUCKS WITH ME! NOBODY FUCKS
WITH ME!* Wasn't that why I chose to do

what I chose to do? And still keep choosing,
still trying to make what I need to make,

to find the way, to do it on my own—
and if nobody hears it, if nobody cares,

whatever comes of it,
at least nobody fucks with me

AUBURNDALE

—Summer 1945

This photo's matte surface feels more alive
than any image a cellphone could provide—

the way its shades of gray vary, the way
sunlight suffuses the mother's pale hair,

the straight dark hair of the boy and girl.
Edenic, a backyard by a river, waterlilies,

mallards, a young mother and her children
the camera clicked and captured, gazing,

entranced, at a litter of gray tiger kittens.
The War's just over, the "victory garden"

overgrown, schoolyard chants,
jump-roping taunts at distant enemies—

I see London, I see France,
I see a hole in Hitler's pants!

—also, almost, over.

Someday, gradually, the children will learn
what happened to their family tree,

but today, the unimaginable erasures
have yet to be discovered,

those distant branches with scratched x's
marking their murdered ones

now, soon to be penciled in—
oh, all dark and comfortless . . .

But here in the yard, beyond the frame,
a rowboat, a wooden dock,

our one American grandparent
sitting in an Adirondack chair

with his fishing pole: paradisial,
pristine, all light yet no real shadows,

just this dappling through the summer willow.

How could there be no shadows visible yet,
only this dappled light, beautiful,

like a blessing manifest?

AFTER PASTORAL

"Go, sit in the woods," I said to myself
in the middle of my life, "and learn
the alphabet for what you can find there."

It was late, but I wanted to change, to *know*
differently, I thought I'd need a new vocabulary,
so I sat, but in the dark, unable to see anything

around me without the right words. I couldn't say
what red ants were like, nesting in mulch and debris,
or the strange (but what wasn't strange?) Indian Pipe

Wampanoags called "ghost plant," white and waxy
Monotropa uniflora, or the brown itch of dead leaves,
the dry acorn caps, the rough bark of a tree at my back.

I sat in a foreign language library wanting it to be
my paradise, I construed nature the way a stunted child
would, without wonder. At first, the Latin names

in my field guide, genus and species, stems and roots,
distracted me from my mission, at home as I was
in the lives of pages, but soon I was trembling

with the indecent pleasure a clever child takes
in spelling, in getting everything right—or the way
my 18-year old grandmother must have felt

in Lincoln, Maine early in the last century,
learning alone each night the math she'd teach
to her ruffians and farm kids the next day

in a one-room schoolhouse in her new land—
each day a triumph, a kind of moral victory
over her own foreignness, her ignorance ....

I walked barefoot down a pine needle path
to the lake and swam with silvery herring minnows
and snappers, I picked wild mint for my tea

and huckleberries with their grainy seeds.
Those summers, I lived in the beech forest,
fagus sylvatica, the final forest, a woman

in mid-life, certain she was growing. A brief chapter,
really, naming the mayflowers—*trailing arbutus*—
and mushrooms, ignoring jet trails and dying pickerel,

uttering what had probably been uttered for eons
in Nature's antique vernaculars. Then, only then,
when I loved it—when I'd begun to be at home in it—

I took my leave ...

HISTORY

What seemed in the living of it shapeless,
now coaxed and tortured into plot....
Our grandparents, *chaff in the wind
to the Tsar*, blundered forward from that place
whose name they were never sure of,

or wouldn't utter—*just the Old Country*—
away from its murderous language, driven
by the twin human needs, to escape and to make—
And I, always goaded by the untold, a kind
of second-story woman, would break and enter....

Years ago I read everyone's childhood streets
and alleys are Edenic in memory, whatever the rubble,
whatever the warp and war of their world—
so, children know to play wherever
they find themselves, rapt in each discovery,

gosling or grenade or four-leaf clover....
The writer who said that may himself have lacked
empathy or imagination, American as he was,
his childhood on a family farm actually *was* Edenic—
but that was "in another country, and besides..."

those weren't our grandparents' stories, their lives
in the new world—the blacksmith, the dentist,
the schoolteacher.... No, from their inheritance
of fear and flight, they aspired to safety, to comfort—
before beauty reached them, before they knew the word

for it, they found Arcadia in this air they breathed....

LUNCH AT THE INSTITUTE AFTER THE ELECTION

I must have been sitting at the wrong table—
the conversation was about chilblains,
someone insisted only the British know
what they are—who among us had had
them, those red eruptions of welts on
hands and feet shivering in the damp cold?
No one.
(I wanted to change the subject so I didn't say
my father had chilblains when he swam
in our icy October lake.) The subject changed,
someone else mentioned an accident she'd had
shortly after 9/11—she'd tripped and fallen
through an iron grate in the East Village,
broken some bones. X asked *What exactly*
is a mongoose? And Y said that word
has no etymological association with the word
"goose"—some live predominantly solitary
lives. Why was I there? Our semester clearly
nearly over. The country, the firmament, all
were changing—yet it seemed nothing was.
Surely, I was sitting at the wrong table,
the conversation turned to butterfly sperm...

MATZOH

As if to mock me in my widowhood,
as if to deride my pandemic isolation,
an enormous carton arrives at my door,
a cosmic error from the Yehuda Matzoh
Company: *ten* boxes, which should last long
enough to get incinerated with me someday
at the venerable New England cemetery
that was once the struggling family farm,
Mount Auburn, of poet Robert Creeley's
great-grandfather, where his descendants
can be buried together *gratis, ad eternam.*
Mirabile dictu, that Bob, the ashes of my beloved,
and mine, will lie close in the pastoral landscape
I like to walk on late spring or early autumn
mornings in the New World's first arboreal
graveyard, a sanctuary, really, for mourners,
bird watchers and my friends the Sunday
botanizers. Will I be buried, or will my ashes
be sprinkled with old dry crumbs of Yehuda's
uncalled-for unrisen bread, to feed the Eastern
Wood-Pewee or the poor Solitary Sandpiper
or the resident loons? Such questions never
arose before, in what we now call *normal times*
when I brought cut flowers to lay on the stone
etched with our names, a palette, a brush,
and pen, nestled nearby the austere markers
of other Jews and Chinese and Armenians,
by Malamud and Achilles Fang and Izzy Stone,
not so near Longfellow and Fannie Farmer or
Mary Baker Eddy and her apocryphal phone,
overlooking a pond that's the serene home
all summer long to a picturesque pair of weeping
willows and two lazy white swans. *Who* on earth

could have been the misinformed deliverer
of such excess to my door, of such harsh symbols
of my people's eternal hardships? Oh, my dear
Yehuda Matzoh, my poor Yehuda Matzoh, how
in your crisp hard plenitude today you ridicule
and tend to amuse me, oh, believe me, I've never
forgotten all the millennia when you've been baked
with the pain and salty tears of my people's exodus—
so yes, I will eat, and eat alone, until the day comes
when I can eat no more of our unleavened bread.

HER STAIRS

> Yesterday, upon the stair,
> I met a man who wasn't there
> He wasn't there again today
> I wish, I wish he'd go away...
>
> from "Antigonish," William Hughes Mearns

A coverless hatbox of
beads and doll parts, a torso, a
pinkish arm, one blue glass eye with-
out eyelashes or a head to roll around in.
A rhinestone brooch, the ruby sparkles gone
from it petals. Three black jet "drop" earrings

in a chipped gravy boat,
beside broken-backed brown
stilettos. Tattered magazines, all of
them, she swears, are "collectible." Eight
tattered albums of old postcards, "treasures":
public parks; fire engines; royal families; "politicals"

*("Gail, Hitlers are worth more
than the king and queen of England!")*
Her stairs an obstacle course of fragments,
narrow terraces of impedimenta, old loose
ends of a drama that's beginning to be forgotten—
and what should I say when she whispers

(the phone's *tapped*) about my cousin
who sneaks in at night to rob her,
he crawls in the dark up from the river?
Her doctor's instructions, not to cross her
always in mind, her shrill voice panicky when
I reason or disagree, so I agree: that *weasel, bottom-*

feeder, trickster hiding somewhere
in her house of afflictions, stealing beets
and string cheese from the refrigerator, thaw-
ing her favorite TV dinners, creeping stealthily
past the eyebeam of the new alarm we had ordered,
slithering viciously under all the padlocked closet doors,

*

stashing her kewpie dolls behind the TV,
moving eyeglasses from the sofa to the toaster
oven, he even separates her salt and pepper shakers,
separates inkwells from the tops, he's age and infirmity
moved in to paralyze her life like a cold Ukrainian winter....
Gail, I need you to do something for me—buy a gun and go

find him and kill him! "But Mom, then I'd go
to prison and I wouldn't fit in—no one would like
me—I'd feel so isolated." I thought that's what writers
want! "No, no, you don't just get to sit all alone in a cell
thinking and writing. I've taught in prisons: you're harassed,
and degraded" (Am I humoring her now or am I crossing over?)"

Yes, and then like Kirk Douglas,
(she hates him) *in that movie, when you*
get out, you couldn't associate with your former
confederates— "But I won't have any confederates, no
one will have anything to do with me because I'd be a murderer—
please don't ask me to kill him." Well, okay, all right, if you say so....

She's got the attic door sealed
with her ingenious improbable mortar,
wet toothpaste and wadded-up toilet paper,
he can't escape, yet like a rat, he evades her:
You shine light into a corner, he darts out of sight.
He's "a cockroach," her criminal boarder, he's blood

of her blood, her hapless nephew,
but that doesn't matter, she's *"walking*
on boils," my once famously beautiful mother,
and he's a ganglion, an ulcer, a malignant tumor,
but she can see I won't believe her, won't make anything
better—plus, she can't walk anymore without the damned walker....

*

I hold to the banister, pick
my way up the carpeted stairs,
I'm on a rescue mission to find some
purloined item—a hairpin, a dresser scarf,
a small hooked rug, one bronze Shakespeare bookend.
I know these old steps, I could still climb them blindfolded,
barefoot, I know what they lead to. I walk in my sleep to their bedroom
door, where I saw my father square his gallant shoulders one last time,
take one last look before he descended for good. And my room,
the twin spool beds I shared with my lost sister now covered
with Buffalo pottery and cardboard cartons of china,
my mother's a hoarder, here are the bookshelves
of tchotchkes, here's all her "ephemera."
On my old night table a crystal chimera
I handle with care, like a safecracker
I feel each ding with trained fingertips. I
caress for a minute the chipped dusty goat body,
the cracked lion head, but I never see what it is I came
for, so I turn back to the stairs and go down empty-handed.

E.R. AT DAWN

What we have in common but do not share—
Love and dread. We just sit here, staring
At the ENTER, ENTRADA door, forbidden
From entering. On the wall TV, tonight's—
No, last night's—World Series final score,
The dead-eyed blank-faced losers stunned,
The jubilant winners dancing.... Almost ready
To celebrate, a young mother doesn't scold
Her small anxious boy, she assures him
"He'll be all right, he'll be all right, have faith."
Then flashing lights of another ambulance.
How to have faith, that golden certainty,
Certainty I try to breathe with and for him.
By my chair, Tuesday's tabloid ripped in half.
In the Ladies Room, bloodied napkins on the floor.

THEN, NOW

We had taken our minds and bodies this far
we'd rid ourselves of our homely baggage

the train's destination was our destination
wherever it would go we'd go

wherever it would stop we'd stop

and however it ended
we too would end

I rested my head on your shoulder
you held my hand

we relived our life
nothing sweet forgotten

then as the day's brief light faded
we arrived here at the place

that for so long seemed a distant station

TWILIGHT AT THE LAKE WITH PAINTER AND CAT

—Mashpee, 1985

Pastel sunset, your easel
facing the darkening lake,
the clear abstracted sky....

Our cat, Mensch, feckless
survivor of ill-matched battles,
dosed with antibiotics,

dozing on my lap. Mashpee.
Life so reduced, yet so various.
We had the amateurs' pride,

"knowing" nature's creatures,
creatures on our short life list
of muskrats, groundhogs, moles,

our limited repertory of birds,
the field guides' elucidations;
we'd sleep with windows open

to the lake's breezes. Mornings,
I'd drive six miles to get the mail.
In it. Not bored, but almost bored—

Outside of time, so we thought.

Three islands, each a swim away,
the Wampanoags named
Come to It, Stay on It, Get Off It.

Nearest to *Come to It*, we'd swim
there, climb to lie in the grassy bed
at the center, tickle each other

gently with the fallen leaves
or pick wild blueberries on *Stay on It*.
Get Off It was all brambly thorns.

Bees, snakes, poison ivy—
at dusk, the untranslatable lucidities
of birds I never thought to memorize

or memorialize those days,
to record or celebrate or regret,
but I did. I do....

Your palette and pastel sticks,
on the weathered porch rail
vying for your favor,

your stance, its familiar absorption....
Rag in your left hand,
instinct in your right, the hand

that all those summers,
all our seasons, captured
the shifting clarities of light....

MIDNIGHT

—Cambridge, 2023

Midnight. My black cat sprints through the kitchen door,
a glassy-eyed cottontail hanging limp from his jaws.

I dread feeling the last flutter of a dying rabbit's heart,
but Bogey wants praise, his city nights peopled

with coyotes, turkeys, rabid raccoons—and bats
high in the sky, silhouetted against the moon . . . .

Midnight. I can't translate the coyotes' howl,
language of passions, soundtrack of sinister cartoons.

But I've become calm, grabbing today's paper
to wrap this plush warm creature, so still,

so *cute*, so *unruffled*, a little calamity lolling here,
its front paws curled, its blood a haiku trickle

on the *Times* front page across Kyiv's savage news.
Looking peaceful at being dead, done with dying.

NOT EKPHRASTIC

People think I'm writing about art
where a poem mentions a painting,

if there's a drawing or sculpture in it,
if I talk about surface, or palette, or mark,

that the poem's purpose is to describe,
feelingly, for a reader, how art works

in the world—or on me. But no,
they're wrong. Whoever thinks *that*

isn't really listening to me.
How *not* understand

where there's art in the poem
I'm talking with you, still talking with you?

RAINY WEDNESDAY

and I'm saying to my students *Don't you have any sense
of privacy?* And oh, they look at me as if I could be one
of their grandmothers which is in fact the case, though
thankfully I am not but I am so discouraged for them
this morning, for their sad lines containing many what
I'd call orifices though orifice is a word if they know it
they'd surely scorn, so they look at me as if I were
speaking Esperanto, thinking it's a universal language
they've not heard tell of, no, they haven't heard of it,
I speak such an antique tongue, oh I would like to speak
of, say, the joys, the fun of bawdiness but they don't know
yet to look *bawdiness* up, they need to be certain in their
inchoate pain that they are being bold with each and every
asshole and cunt and cock, nakednesses they're haven't yet
any idea how to *play* with, denatured, and oh deadened
organs. Don't I understand, they say, or seem to, writers
should have no sense of privacy? I am absurd, antique,
their *no-o-o* in unison is so—so *choral*—so sadly sure
of its group self in the fluoresced classroom—am I alone
here honoring the beautiful old bards and the mad ones,
those dear ecstatics, oh brave heartbreakers, oh beloved
songmakers, dear geniuses of history, we won't despair,
it's pouring outside, soon another class will be coming....

ICE GLEN

Ice Glen, a side trip on our trip
to see old friends. Our plan,
a hike, and then there was the thought
of Hawthorne and Melville,
a century earlier, and *their* friends,
sitting on boulders singing,
drinking, and "telling tales," calling
across the romantic mossed abyss—
we knew their incipient romance
crashed and burned.... Steamy
August afternoon in Stockbridge,
the sun above us a round flame.
Romantic to have thought of hiking up,
then down to the ravine, the icy chasm
someone once called *a curious fissure*.
Might it be like a bottomless well
we'd each drop a wishing stone into?
We only got close. What you saw there
you saw with your inner eye, a radiance;
what I saw was unfathomable, sunless.
Frigid, frosted, the air that turned us back—
too cold for us, but we were laughing
as we fled to Main Street. Cold,
but I wish our two souls were there now
together in that dappled underworld.

DON'T SPEAK OF HEARTBREAK

Don't speak of heartbreak to me—I have an argument

It was April, I brought him pale tulips from the garden

with habits of metaphor—it's not the heart you speak of
but the ineffable—character, soul, courage,

With my pen, he drew pages of ravishing faltering tulips

locus of feeling. Don't tell me a muscle's made whole
by breaking, made stronger ravaged and repaired.

brought me the too-muchness of the Asiatic lily's perfume

How could we salvage joy (as if the heart lives

His hand transfigured the pure white paper
to a garden room—Edenic opulent various alive

by breaking) from our savage grief?

LOW TIDE

At a loss today for what to do
I walk out onto the flats
which do appear

reliably when the tides
predictably go out, a true fact
I've learned ridiculously late in life

because I grew up on a river. Now
in warm morning sunlight,
at mid-day or evening,

the world's still changing,
fluctuating, so much unpredictable....
and when I'm at a loss, these particulars

of life renewing in tidal pools help
me forget what I've lost
so I read odd

calligraphic messages
small invisible creatures leave
in their quickening travels along the sand,

I follow a minnow's rhythmic wriggles,
ribboning trails of sea worms whose
genus I keep unlearning,

of hermit crabs dragging
newly abandoned homes heavily
across the wet sands, always on the look-out

for more capacious, more hospitable
emptied shells. Ceramic sand-
scoured shards of cast-off

plates, or bottles once tossed
off long lost ships, their wet sheen
frosted beautifully by the tide's abrasions,

the bowl of a white clay pipe, old flotsam
gifts of another century's shipwreck
still returning, emblems of our

obscure histories. Now, a sweet
wonderment of spotting my friend Marion
this late September morning in her *navasana*

pose on a neighbor's deck, her cotton shirt
luminous, her smile beatific, two of us
at peace in the universe we share...

UNVEILING IN SNOW

Because you and I never did sit on a park bench
chatting, or strolled happily along rowdy city streets
browsing or hopscotched chalked sidewalks together,

or read the same articles or books; and because
in our so-called adult lives, we never sang together
except *all* of us at family birthdays; never said things

that professed *love*; also because, though for years
we shared our childhood bedroom, the twin spool beds
our mother doggedly sanded and refinished, we didn't—

that I remember—share jokes or sisterly confidences;
because I was the elder, I, who unwittingly determined
what we *were* together—we were more separate

in our bond than our differences made inevitable;
because together we weathered the tempests
of our mother's house—*because because because*

because I can't say the cause, these words I keep to myself
this raw February day your stone's unveiled—I,
the sister, this Gail who tried to exonerate herself then,

still tries to forgive herself now.

I'd probably have given her two minutes that Monday evening. I was on my way out to a reading. What poet was reading, I don't remember. Since then, I've tried not to regret not letting her phone ring longer. I assumed naturally she was ignoring it—or holding on to doorknobs struggling to get to it, to haul her tottering little body from her kitchen to the den she 'd been living in for a decade.

No answering machine, no computer there, or cable, just the TV on around the clock—three channels of lively familiar tedium.

Her reaction to 9/11, to 24-hours-a-day footage of the towers imploding, of live bodies falling, bodies incinerated, the devastation, its implications: indifference? She didn't want to hear about it— according to her, I was sentimental, soft.

What moved her? She could decide when something moved her—and it would never move her to tears.

She worried about her stocks. New Yorkers were alien to her, without gentility or finesse. Aggressive. *Rotten.* The Empire State building had gone up when she was in Girls' Latin School swooning over Cicero and Shakespeare and the history of England. Her sweet walk home along Huntington Ave then had been "all book stalls." Idyllic. *Golden days.*

The day before, I'd walked from mid-town to "Ground Zero," the numb somber world of it, strange smell of it, wondering what would change, what wouldn't. Apocalyptic, I'd thought, no new word for it. The mayor—"America's mayor" (now, just another creep)— had asked us all to shop, most stores were open, so I bought socks, bought cords for our devices.

There was no thing to want, really . . . .

And I'd been relieved she didn't share our animal bewilderment and terror, the grief that seized us. To her, what happened could have happened on another planet. She'd just switch channels, there'd always be Perry Mason and Della Street somewhere....

I'd come home too late to try calling again.

The next morning, the hockey coach who lived next door phoned to tell me she'd "collapsed"—he'd knocked, then seen her through the kitchen window, on the floor, and called 911. Then, me. I didn't ask him anything, just sped the 8 miles to my childhood home. On Kingswood Road an ambulance was moving silently away, no siren screaming. No patient, I thought, no life-saving care.

At my mother's dining room table, two policemen were searching her old leather purse for information. *Are you the daughter?* There'd been no rush to Emergency. I could see she'd died cooking, her crumpled body on the kitchen floor, a wooden spoon in her hand. I think she'd have liked that, to have died stirring. Maybe when I was calling. The daughter. Her pot of stew had blackened.

Little body, little clump of clothes, my blue-eyed mother face down on the linoleum floor, a ladle still in your hand.

I didn't turn her over to see her expression, or if her nose was broken—she'd have hated that, the way she'd hate my writing this. But I studied the scene like a detective. I found no "signs of struggle," no evidence she'd tried to move, or cried out; no indication she'd been conscious when she fell.

Then the cops left, satisfied her death was from "natural causes." The coach's wife brought over bagels and coffee. I was grateful, I admired her tact—had there ever been a bagel in any house on Kingswood Road except ours?

My brother came, my sister, and Levine's came, respectful of our privacy (they'd buried our father, they had a file on us—back then, they'd said to me, *Your mother, may she live a hundred years....*).They draped her with a white sheet the size of one of her Sunday tablecloths, plain but for the blue Star of David. We followed the gurney over the cracked front walk to the hearse, the beginning of the end of our following.

Little death, I thought then, so singular and so ordinary, and in my hollow ear I heard her voice, speaking clear and firm, saying definitely to me, You did as well as you could—all I could ask for, considering our story. And what went with you, Mother—all the cutting, the stirring and the broiling, the pinches added, the straining, the spicy goulash, the meatloaves, the blintzes, the pies, the forgiving and also the unforgiving, the sweet and bitter peppery stew of your life, and I'd partaken of it all along, my mother, and I was fed—

POEMS

I've made them, but like children
they've stopped being mine—

what then are they made *of?*
Not flesh, not sinew, not blood

though they live here in me,
even after I've sent them away.

Look: I can put my hand on one,
they're always near. Not ivory,

not hair and bone, not fur.
Not neat, messy really.

Not warm. But still, not cold.

Not clear glass, though they do want
to be polished, they expect to shine.

Always near me, *mine*—

yet for how long?

When do they sneak off to separate lives,
to live on their own, hungry or sated?

How will they do? Where do they think
they're going without me?

CONVERSATION

To the artist there is never anything ugly in nature.

—Rodin

When you were five, your father took you and your new toy sailboat to the "pond" in Central Park and photographed his little curly-haired boy kneeling at the pool's edge, your immaculate suspendered shorts and pristine white shirt, as you solemnly coaxed the pristine boat to move. All around you, outside the picture's scalloped edges, the Park's great encyclopedia of trees, is waiting for you to learn to read.

*

In your drawing, so scorched, were these oaks, so naked, still alive? Were their roots entangled deep in the earth so they were one organism, one family alive, as it looks on this page, their branches reaching out, involved, touching each other?

*

At your easel, your sticks of charcoal, that fierce black what you needed—could they, too, have been oak? On the ground, the kneaded eraser, lumpy, already blackened.

*

These trees, I think, so stripped, so powerful, so tenacious—Gail, I remind myself, they're not metaphors, they're trees.

*

Charcoal in your hand, and so connected to the burnt trees, as if the fire that blackened them birthed the charcoal stick in your hand.

**

You loved what you called "the spikiness of forms." These branches.

*

You loved art so much you even loved ekphrastic poems, which I always thought were over-determined, "projects."

*

You loved Peter Watkins' film about Edvard Munch, especially hearing the magnified sound of his brush on canvas as "Munch" painted his dying sister, Sophie. I think you loved being in the blackened theater with the sounds of your studio. You never wanted to be far from art-making. You were multilingual, you and the trees, you knew each others' languages, without study, without guides. That day you knew all you needed to know about each other. In their limbs, in the limbic, you understood each other. Your wordless conversation, the three of them and you.

**

Three of them magnificent, multilingual, operatic—but as Bachelard would say, "More magnificent, the sublime and moving space between them."

KOREN

—in memory of Ed Koren and Michael Mazur

Today in *The New Yorker*
a "new" cartoon
by your old friend Ed,
gone now over a year.
It's a poetry reading
by the Grim Reaper,
a squiggly scratchy Koren
ghoul in the front row
saying *"His poetry is good
but a little dark."* Oh Ed,
oh Mike, alone here
at our kitchen table
I'm eating a turkey
(a Thanksgiving leftover)
sandwich, not wanting
to turn the page
on *The New Yorker*
cartoon. *"His poetry,"*
the creature says, *"is good—
but a little dark..."*
At 16, you two invented
your school's first Art
Club, with Henry Geldzahler,
who became a curator,
pal of Warhol and Hockney.
It's winter.
I'm eating a sandwich
alone at our kitchen table.
In Ed's cartoon, the reaper's
standing at the podium,
and the beaky-nosed creature

is still commenting,
*"His poetry is good but
a little dark."* The school
in Riverdale had never had
an art club before. Oh, boys,
today at this table, eating
my sandwich, I don't want
to turn the page....

ACKNOWLEDGMENTS

I am grateful to the editors of these journals, in which some of these poems appeared: *Battery Journal*, *Harvard Review*, *Peripheries*, *Ploughshares*, *Plume*, *Poem-a-Day*, *Revel*, *Salamander*, and *Salmagundi*.

"Three Trees" appears in *The Map of Every Lilac Leaf: Poets Respond to the Smith College Museum of Art*.

GAIL MAZUR is the author of nine books of poetry, including *Nightfire*; *The Pose of Happiness*; *The Common*, *They Can't Take that Away from Me*, finalist for the National Book Award; *Zeppo's First Wife: New and Selected Poems*, winner of the Massachusetts Book Prize and finalist for the Los Angeles Times Book Prize and the Paterson Poetry Prize; *Figures in a Landscape*; *Forbidden City*; *Land's End: New and Selected Poems*; and *World on a String*. Her poems have been widely anthologized, including in several Pushcart Prize anthologies, the Best American Poetry series, and Robert Pinsky's *Essential Pleasures*.

She has received fellowships from the National Endowment for the Arts, the Bunting Institute of Radcliffe College, and the Radcliffe Institute. The founding director of The Blacksmith House Poetry Series, she has taught at Boston University, Emerson College, and elsewhere, and served for many years on the Writing Committee of the Fine Arts Work Center in Provincetown.

BOOKS BY

ARROWSMITH⟫⊢
PRESS

Girls by Oksana Zabuzhko

Bula Matari/Smasher of Rocks by Tom Sleigh

This Carrying Life by Maureen McLane

Cries of Animals Dying by Lawrence Ferlinghetti

Animals in Wartime by Matiop Wal

Divided Mind by George Scialabba

The Jinn by Amira El-Zein

Bergstein
edited by Askold Melnyczuk

Arrow Breaking Apart by Jason Shinder

Beyond Alchemy by Daniel Berrigan

Conscience, Consequence: Reflections on Father Daniel Berrigan
edited by Askold Melnyczuk

Ric's Progress by Donald Hall

Return To The Sea by Etnairis Rivera

The Kingdom of His Will by Catherine Parnell

Eight Notes from the Blue Angel by Marjana Savka

Fifty-Two by Melissa Green

Music In—And On—The Air by Lloyd Schwartz

Magpiety by Melissa Green

Reality Hunger by William Pierce

Soundings: On The Poetry of Melissa Green
edited by Sumita Chakraborty

The Corny Toys by Thomas Sayers Ellis

Black Ops by Martin Edmunds

Museum of Silence by Romeo Oriogun

City of Water by Mitch Manning

Passeggiate by Judith Baumel

Persephone Blues by Oksana Lutsyshyna

The Uncollected Delmore Schwartz
edited by Ben Mazer

The Light Outside by George Kovach

The Blood of San Gennaro by Scott Harney
edited by Megan Marshall

No Sign by Peter Balakian

Firebird by Kythe Heller

The Selected Poems of Oksana Zabuzhko
edited by Askold Melnyczuk

The Age of Waiting by Douglas J. Penick

Manimal Woe by Fanny Howe

Crank Shaped Notes by Thomas Sayers Ellis

The Land of Mild Light by Rafael Cadenas
edited by Nidia Hernández

The Silence of Your Name: The Afterlife of a Suicide by Alexandra Marshall

Flame in a Stable by Martin Edmunds

Mrs. Schmetterling by Robin Davidson

This Costly Season by John Okrent

Thorny by Judith Baumel

The Invisible Borders of Time: Five Female Latin American Poets
edited by Nidia Hernández

Some of You Will Know by David Rivard

The Forbidden Door: The Selected Poetry of Lasse Söderberg
tr. by Lars Gustaf Andersson & Carolyn Forché

Unrevolutionary Times by Houman Harouni

Between Fury & Peace: The Many Arts of Derek Walcott
edited by Askold Melnyczuk

The Burning World by Sherod Santos

Today is a Different War: Poetry of Lyudmyla Khersonska
tr. by Olga Livshin, Andrew Janco, Maya Chhabra, & Lev Fridman

Salvage by Richard Kearney

In the Hour of War: Poetry From Ukraine
edited by Carolyn Forché and Ilya Kaminsky

A Crash Course in Molotov Cocktails: Poetry of Halyna Kruk
tr. by Amelia Glaser and Yuliya Ilchuk

Don't Close Your Eyes by Hanna Melnyczuk

Tiny Extravaganzas by Diane Mehta

Departures from Rilke by Steven Cramer

On the Road to Lviv by Christopher Merrill
tr. into Ukrainian by Nina Murray

Nothing Bad Has Ever Happened
A Bouquet to Victoria Amelina

The Farewell Light by Nidia Hernández

Downfall of the Straight Line by Charles O. Hartman

The God of Freedom by Yulia Musakovska
tr. Olena Jennings and the author

Away Away by Mark Pawlak

The Miró Worm and the Mysteries of Writing by Sven Birkerts

St. Matthew Passion by Gjertrud Schnackenberg

ARROWSMITH is named after the late William Arrowsmith, a renowned classics scholar, literary and film critic. General editor of thirty-three volumes of *The Greek Tragedy in New Translations*, he was also a brilliant translator of Eugenio Montale, Cesare Pavese, and others. Arrowsmith, who taught for years in Boston University's University Professors Program, championed not only the classics and the finest in contemporary literature, he was also passionate about the importance of recognizing the translator's role in bringing the original work to life in a new language.

Like the arrowsmith who turns his arrows straight and true,
a wise person makes his character straight and true. —Buddha

www.ingramcontent.com/pod-product-compliance
Lightning Source LLC
Chambersburg PA
CBHW020422150626
46554CB00014B/2365